LEVEL D

A King on a Swing

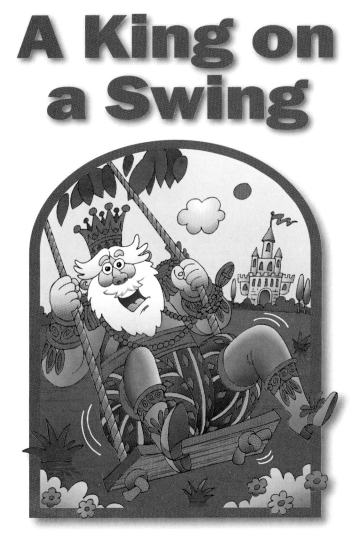

by Donald Rasmussen and Lynn Goldberg

Columbus, Ohio

A Division of The **McGraw·Hill** Companies

SRA/McGraw-Hill

A Division of The **McGraw·Hill** *Companies*

Send all inquiries to:
SRA/McGraw-Hill
8787 Orion Place
Columbus, OH 43240

Printed in the United States of America.

ISBN 0-02-684002-2

 2 3 4 5 6 7 8 9 0 RRC 05 04 03 02 01

Illustrator:

Devere Appleyard

Contributors:

Ann Bishop
Justin M. Fishbein
Mary Virginia Fox
Emery Hutchison
Kay W. Levin
Annie Moldafsky
Bonnie Nims
George R. Paterson
Enid Warner Romanek
John Savage

Contents

Section 1

word lists 1

sentences 3

A King on a Swing 4

The Jumping Frog 6

Fran at Camp 13

Why the King Went to Bed 23

Bing Bang Band 24

The Big Fat Mess 25

Section 2

word lists 33

sentences 34

The Junkman's Skunk 36

The Junkman's Trunk 37

Jan Elf 43

Ink Spot 52

Mrs. Kent's Trip 54

Section 3

word lists 64

sentences 65

A Snack for a Cat 67

Said a Duck 74

The Gruff King 75

A Fresh Fish for Two 82

Mrs. Bly Helps an Elf 83

Section 4

word lists 92

sentences 93

The Fish and the Bat 94

I Think I'll Be 104

Dad's Rest 105

The Thing That Went Bump 112

This and That 117

Who's Who? 120

Section 5

word lists 122

sentences 123

Cat in the Jam Pot 125

What's for Lunch? 128

Chip Is My Chum 134

Jet and His Pal 135

Shopping for Fun 143

What Is an Inch? 156

Section 6

word lists 158

sentences 160

Ann Gets the Milk 161

The Clock. 168

What Can You Do? 169

Miss Quick-Quack 171

_ng				
bang		king		hung
gang		ring		lung
hang		sing		rung
rang		wing		sung
sang		bring		clung
clang		cling		stung
		sting		swung
		swing		

_ing

banging hanging clanging ■ camping	resting testing ■ melting	ringing singing bringing clinging stinging swinging ■ lifting sifting ■ wilting		hunting ■ jumping

_ing

batting ■ clapping	sledding ■ stepping	digging ■ swimming	dropping stopping	running

isn't
∎
aren't
∎
wasn't
∎
weren't
∎
couldn't
wouldn't
shouldn't
∎
hadn't
∎
hasn't
∎
haven't
∎
didn't
∎
mustn't

Tim and his pals <u>hadn't</u> anything to do.

"<u>Haven't</u> you got any plans?" said Tim.

"We could put on a skit," said Tim's pal, Jim.

But Tim <u>wasn't</u> for that. He said he <u>couldn't</u> act. He <u>didn't</u> want to clap, and he <u>wouldn't</u> yell. They <u>weren't</u> the things he had fun at.

Tim's pal said, "Tim just <u>hasn't</u> got any pep."

But Tim said, "It <u>isn't</u> that. But it's hot, and I want to swim. <u>Aren't</u> you hot?"

"Yes," said Jim, "but we <u>shouldn't</u> swim in the pond. Sam's mom said we <u>mustn't</u>."

A King on a Swing

Cling-clang-cling! Cling-clang-cling!
The bell began to ring.
"We want the king."
But he was on a swing.
Cling-clang-cling! Cling-clang-cling!

"Wing-a-zing-a-zing!
If I am the king,
Why shouldn't I swing
As I sit and sing?
Wing-a-zing-a-zing!"

"Ting-a-ling-ling!
You are a king!
You must not sing!
You must not swing!
Ting-a-ling-ling!"

"Wing-a-zing-a-zing!
Let's have the bell ring.
For it's fun to sing.
And it's fun to swing!
Wing-a-zing-a-zing!"

Cling-a-clang-clinging,
The bell is still ringing.
The swing is still swinging!
The king is still singing,
Still wing-a-zing-zinging!

5

The Jumping Frog

Ann was yelling as she ran back from
the pond. "I have it! I have it!"
she kept on yelling.

"What are you bringing in the can?"
said Ann's dad.

"I have a frog," Ann said. "I got it
just as it was hopping onto a rock by
the pond. It's a big jumping frog!"

"O, it IS a big frog," said Dad.
"You must get a box so the frog cannot
jump back to the pond. Did Max help
you get it?"

"No, Dad, I got it by myself. And I
have a box for the frog next to my bed."

"You must have had fun at the pond,"
said Dad.

"I did. But I want to have a rest.
I got up at six o'clock to go to the
pond," said Ann. And off she went to
bed, still clinging to the can.

Ann put the frog into the box and got
into bed. She left the box on the rug
by the bed. Ann was resting but the
frog wasn't. Bing! Bang! Clang! The
frog was jumping in the box. It didn't
want to rest.

Bang! Pop! The lid fell off the box
and the frog was jumping on the rug.

Zing! The frog was sitting on Ann's
bed. Hop! It was on Ann herself. Ann
got up swinging and kicking. Bang!
She hit her clock and it fell. As it
fell, it went ring-a-ding-ding, and it
did not stop.

The frog kept on jumping. Next it was
on Ann's desk. It began slipping. Bump!
Bang! It slid into the desk lamp.

"O! No!" said Ann. But she could not
get to the lamp and it fell, banging on
the rug.

Ann got up from her bed and began to grab at the frog. But the frog kept hopping and jumping from the bed to the desk and back to the bed.

Ann said, "I know what to do! I will trap the frog." So Ann got a net and hid in back of her desk. The frog was hopping and jumping on and off the bed. Ann sat as still as she could. Just as the frog got past the desk, Ann swung her net. But just as Ann swung her net, Dad ran in to ask what the bumping was. The net hit Dad on his legs and upset him. He fell huffing and puffing on the rug next to the frog. The frog didn't know what to do! So Ann swung the net on top of it.

"Get it! Grab it!" said Dad. "Put it in the box. I have the lid."

Ann held the frog on its back and slid it into the box. Bang! Dad put the lid on. At last the frog was still and Dad and Ann could rest.

"Ann," said Dad, "your frog wants to jump. It can't jump in a box, can it?"

"No," said Ann.

"And it wants to go swimming," said Dad.

"It can't swim in the box," said Ann.

"The frog will have to have many, many bugs," said Dad, "and we haven't got many for him here."

"The frog should go back to the pond, shouldn't it?" said Ann.

"Yes," said Dad. "Will you bring it back and let it go?"

Ann would have said O.K. But she couldn't. She was napping.

Fran at Camp

Fran and her gang were at camp at last. They sang and said they were going to have fun.

Nan ran off to the dock.

Ann began to go up to the hilltop.

Pam went digging in the sand.

14

"Cling-clang, cling-clang," rang the big camp bell. It rang to let Fran and her pals know they could go swimming.

It was so hot they were glad the swimming bell had rung. They went to dress for swimming. The pals met in the tent.

"Fran isn't here," said Nan.

"The bell will bring her," said Ann.

They were set to go, but Fran still hadn't come. Pam and Nan began to yell, "Fran, come here! We want to go swimming."

"Do you want to miss your swim?" Ann was yelling at the top of her lungs.

Still Fran didn't come.

"Is Fran sitting on top of the hill?" said Pam.

"Is she digging in the sand by the pond?" said Ann.

"Is she swinging on the swings?" said Jill.

"Could she be sunning herself on the dock?" said Nan.

"Let's hunt for her," said Pam.

"Let's go to the swings," said Jill.

"And to the dock and the pond," said Nan.

"And up the hill," said Pam.

As they were hunting they went by a big tan tent. It was the sick tent—a tent for camp pals who were ill.

"We are hunting for Fran," Ann said to a man sitting next to the tent. The man was Doc Kling.

"Did Fran come past here?" said Jill.

"She didn't come PAST here," said Doc Kling. "She is IN here."

Fran was in a bed at the back of the
tent. Her gang began to yell at her,
"Get up! Get up! It's hot in the
tent. Let's go swimming!"

But Doc Kling said, "No! No!
You mustn't yell at Fran. And you
mustn't go in," he went on. "She is sick.
She has the mumps and can't go
swimming. She has to rest in bed."

The gang was sad. Fran was sick.
She wasn't going to have any fun in
camp.

"Why don't you go swimming?" said
Doc Kling. "I don't want the rest of
you to get the mumps."

They went to the pond. But they
were so sad they didn't want to swim.
They just sat on the sand. They didn't
know what to do to help Fran. "Let's get
her some gifts," said Jill.

At sunset, as the last bell rang, the gang went to the sick tent.

"Your pals are bringing you some gifts," said Doc Kling.

Pam had a bag of plums. Nan had a red cup for Fran's milk. Jill had a get-well ring.

Fran began to grin. "I can't go swimming or running or skipping," she said. "But I can have fun here. It is not so bad to be sick at camp if your pals help you get well."

Why the King Went to Bed

An ant stung the king

As he swung on his swing,

And the sting was so bad,

   The king bled.

"Stop the swing!" said the king,

"I'm so sick from the sting,

I can't stand it—

   I'm going to bed!"

Bing Bang Band

Bring your drum
  And you can bang it——
Bing-bang-banging,
    BANG BANG BANG!

Bring a can
  And you can clang it——
Cling-clang-clanging,
    CLANG CLANG CLANG!

Bring a bell
  And you can ring it——
Ting-ting-a-linging,
    DING DING DING!

The Big Fat Mess

Mrs. Kent got into a cab. "I must go
fast, Mr. Cabman!" she said. "I want
to go to Miss West's, at 606 Crabgrass.
Go as fast as you can."

The cab began to go fast, but it got
stuck.

"It's a flat," the cabman said, stopping.

And so the mess began. The cab was tilting and tipping. But the cabman just sat.

"Shouldn't you be going for help?" said Mrs. Kent. "Shouldn't you go up the block to get help?"

But the cabman just said, "What a mess! What a mess!"

A milk truck went skidding by. It had to zigzag past the cab. It began dropping cans of milk. The cans were rocking and clanging and spilling. A big cat began sniffing the milk and licking it up. His six pals ran up to help him.

Mrs. Kent said, "Couldn't you get help, Mr. Cabman?"

But still the cabman just sat. "What a
mess!" he said. "What a mess!"

A red bus slid in the milk. The bus was
slipping and skidding, and it ran into a
van. The van began to tip. The van had
pop and buns and hotdogs in it. The pop
fell off the van. It began popping and
fizzing. The buns fell off and got wet.
So did the hotdogs. Some pups ran up.

The pups began to snap at the hotdogs. It was a mess. It was a BIG mess!

Mrs. Kent began to get upset. "Why won't you get help?" she said. "Aren't you going to fix the flat? Why do you just sit?"

But the cabman just sat. "What a mess!" he said. "What a mess, mess, mess!"

Yes, it was a big mess. It was a big FAT mess! Pop was fizzing. Milk was running. Cats were lapping and gulping! Buns sat in lumps and hotdogs in humps. Pups were tripping in milk and flopping in pop! The bus man was yelling at the van man.

The van man was yelling at the cats and pups.

"It's bad," said Mrs. Kent. "It's a bad, bad mess, Mr. Cabman."

"Why tell ME?" the cabman said. "Why tell ME it's bad? I was just doing my job. I didn't bang the van. I didn't bring the cats. I didn't dump the buns. I didn't spill the milk. I didn't pop the pop. I was just doing my job and BANG—I had a flat. Don't tell me! It isn't MY mess!"

"But you COULD go for help," said Mrs. Kent.

The cabman felt glum. "Who would help us?" he said. "Who?"

At last Mrs. Kent got mad. She began yelling!

"YOU, is who! YOU get going, Mr. Cabman! Stop sitting and get mopping! And you, Mr. Bus Man! Stop napping and grab the pups! Scat the cats! And you, Mr. Van Man! Stop nodding and bag the buns! Pick up the hotdogs! Sop up the pop! Get going! As for me, I will fix the flat."

Well, they did. They weren't glad to do it, but Mrs. Kent didn't let them stop. And she did fix the flat.

Fixing a flat is a mess of a job. So Mrs. Kent's dress was a mess. The van man and the bus man were huffing and puffing. And the cabman still felt glum.

Then Mrs. Kent began to grin. And she began to sing. She sang:

"Get going, get going, get going!
Lend a hand! It's a big fat mess!
   Mop, mop, mop up the slop!
   Sop, sop, sop up the pop!
   Yell scat, scat at a cat!
   And let me fix the flat!
Get going, get going, get going!
Lend a hand! It's a big fat mess!"

As Mrs. Kent sang, the van man began to grin, and the bus man began to grin. And at last the cabman himself began to grin!

And the van man, the bus man, and the cabman began to sing:

"We did it, we did it, we did it!
It's the end of the big fat mess!"

And it was!

bank		pink		bunk
Hank		sink		dunk
rank		wink		hunk
sank		blink		junk
tank		clink		sunk
yank		drink		clunk
blank				skunk
clank				drunk
crank				trunk
drank				
Frank				

he'd	he'll	he's			
we'd	we'll		we're	we've	
she'd	she'll	she's	■	■	
■	■				
I'd	I'll			I've	I'm
■	■			■	
they'd	they'll		they're	they've	
■	■		■	■	
you'd	you'll		you're	you've	

"We're going camping," Tom said to Pat. "Dad is going and so are his pals. And he said we could come. He's got to pack. He'll bring the tent and I'll help him."

"Is Mom coming?" Pat said.

"Yes, she's coming. She'll run the van. Let's get some snacks."

"We'll want some milk," said Pat.

"We've put some in," said
Tom. "And Dad said we'd bring eggs.
His pals said they'd bring a ham."

"I've got to get the bags," said
Pat. "Dad and his pals will have a lot
to do at camp. They'll have to set up
the tents. I'm going swimming."

"You're going to help them. Dad
said you'd lend a hand," Tom said.

"O.K.," said Pat. "They're here!
Let's go."

"I'm set," Tom said. "Come on.
Here's Dad. We're off!"

The Junkman's Skunk

The junkman's skunk will sit and beg
For nuts and snacks and drinks,
And if the junkman picks her up,
She nods at him and winks.

She's kept in a pen on the junkman's truck,
And she drinks from a pink tin cup,
Her bed is just a big flat plank
The junkman has put up.

The junkman lets me pet his skunk
And fix her snacks and drinks,
But she won't nod or wink at ME:
She just sits still and blinks.

The Junkman's Trunk

Cast:
Hank
Fran
The Junkman

Hank: Here comes the junk truck, Fran.

Fran: A big box fell off the truck!

Hank: It's a trunk. Let's tell him.

Fran and Hank (yelling): Mr. Junkman!
   Stop!

Junkman (stopping his truck): What is it?

Hank: A trunk fell off your truck.

Junkman: It's just got junk in it, but I'll
go back and get it. It has to go to
the dump.

Fran: You're going to dump it?

Junkman: Yes.

Hank: What's the junk in it?

Junkman: Just hunks of junk: a clock — it
can go clink-clank but it won't run.
A drum — a tent — some bells and stuff.

Fran: What swell stuff! I wouldn't junk
it if I were you! I'd want to have it.

Junkman: Not me. I'm dumping it.

Hank: Can WE have it?

Fran: Yes, can we have it if you don't
want it?

Junkman: You could. But you wouldn't
want it.

Hank and Fran: Yes we would! We do!

Junkman: No you wouldn't. You don't.

Hank: But we DO want it. We wouldn't tell
you we want it if we didn't want it.

Junkman: O.K., you want it. And I'd be
glad to let you have it, but . . .

Hank: You will!

Junkman: I said I'd be GLAD to. But you're
not going to want it if you get it.

Hank: Why not?

Junkman: Well, the junk . . .

Fran: It's not junk — not to us! It's swell
stuff and will be a lot of fun for us.

Junkman: But the junk in the trunk has . . .

Hank: Not junk!

Junkman: WILL you let me tell you . . .

Fran: O! Mr. Junkman, don't be a crank.

    If you don't let us have the trunk,

    we'll be so sad!

Junkman: Well, you pests won't let me tell

    you, and I can't go on gabbing and

    fussing. So O.K.

    (He runs off and brings the trunk back.)

    You've got it. It's yours. I BET you'll

    have fun!

    (He grins and winks and clanks off

    in his truck.)

Hank: We've got the trunk, Fran!

Fran and Hank: It's swell of you, Mr. Junkman!

Junkman (yelling back): Don't tell me it's

    swell till you get the lid off.

Fran: It has a lock!

Hank: Yes, but we can get it off if we get

a rock and hit it.

Fran: Here's a rock, Hank. Bang it!

Clang it! Clunk it!

Hank: I'm banging. I'm clanging. I'm

clunking. I'm getting it.

Fran: Can't you yank it off?

Hank: I'm yanking. And it's off!

(The lid comes off the trunk. The

stuff spills from it.)

Fran and Hank: Ick! Ack! Uck! Help!

(They run back from the trunk.)

Fran: It smells! It smells as if a skunk

had got into it!

Hank: That's it! A skunk HAS got
into it. The junkman has a pet
skunk. It must have got into the
trunk and got mad or upset. Skunks
don't smell till they get mad. But if
they do get mad they'll put up a fuss.
Well, we know why the junkman was
dumping this trunk!

Fran: I'm getting sick from the smell.
(They begin to run.) Let's get going!

Hank: But why didn't the junkman tell us?
He should know we wouldn't want it.

Fran: He DID know, Hank. And he was going
to tell us. But we wouldn't let him!

THE END

Jan Elf

A jug hung on a rack next to some
pots and pans. The jug had a nest in it.
In the nest were Mom, Jan, Frank, and
Nell Elf.

Mom Elf said to Jan, Frank, and
Nell, "I'm going to get some
milk to drink. You must sit here in
the jug. Be still and rest."

Frank and Nell Elf said, "Yes, Mom. We'll sit. We'll rest—and have some fun—in the jug."

"Not me!" said Jan Elf. "I don't want to rest. I want to jump and run. I can't jump and run here in the jug. It isn't any fun in here. I'm big! I want to go!"

But Mom Elf said, "No, no, Jan. You're not big yet. You mustn't go."

Jan Elf was sad. But Mom Elf left. She went skipping off to get the milk.

Nell Elf got into her bunk bed, and in a wink she was napping. But Jan Elf did not nap. She got up to the neck of the jug.

"Jan Elf, you come back!" said Frank. "You know that mother will be mad."

Jan Elf sat on the neck of the jug and said to herself, "At last! At last! At last I can run and jump!" Plunk! She had left the jug.

She was next to a pot and a big pan.

"O well! I can't run, but I can still have fun," she said to herself.

And she began to swing on the big pot next to her. Clink! Clunk! She swung up and back. She clung to the rim of the pot. What a prank! What fun! "I can swing and I know I won't slip," Jan said.

But she DID slip.

Flip! Flop! Plip! Plop!

Jan Elf was in the pot. And the pot had red plum jam in it!

"I must swim," Jan Elf said to herself. But she couldn't. She was sinking fast.

She sank till she was up to her neck in jam.

"I know what I'll do," she said. "I'll jump and jump till I can grab the rim of the pot. If I can cling to it, I can get back onto the lid."

Plip! Plop! She did it!

Jan Elf was limping as she went back
to the jug. Her steps were sticking,
and jam was dripping from her back.
A sad Jan Elf went up to the jug.

Bang! Bang! Bang!

Jan Elf began banging on the jug.
"I'm back! I'm back! Let me in!
It's Jan Elf. Let me in!"

Mom Elf went up to the top of the
jug. She began to blink.

"Who are you?" she said. "I don't
know you. Jan Elf is not red, so you
can't be my Jan. You're as red as
a plum. You must be JAM ELF!"
And she wouldn't let Jan Elf come in!

Bad Jan Elf was sad. If her
mom didn't know her, what could
she do?

She began banging and hitting the jug.
She said, "I am NOT Jam Elf. I am Jan—
your elf."

But Mom Elf still wouldn't let
her in. She went back into the jug.

Jan Elf said to herself, "I must
get rid of the jam. If I don't, Mom
won't know who I am. She won't
let me back into the jug."

So Jan Elf got a rag. She got some
of the jam off by rubbing herself.
And she got rid of the rest of the
jam by licking herself. She didn't
have any jam left on her. But she had
a lot of jam IN her.

"I'm sick of plum jam!" she said.
"If my Mom will let me in, I'll sit
on my bunk in the jug and I
won't run off."

Jan Elf went back to the jug.
She got Mom Elf to let her in
by banging on it.

Grinning, Mom Elf said, "I'm glad
you're back, Jan. Run off to the sink.
Will you have some jam and some
milk to drink?"

Mom, Nell, and Frank Elf
were glad to have Jan Elf back.
Jan was glad to be back. But
Jan did not want any jam.

Ink Spot

Ink Spot the skunk
Was a swell pet for Bill.
Ink Spot was fun,
But he wouldn't sit still.

He'd yank at the rugs.
He'd dig up odd junk.
He'd slink off for bugs.
He had lots of spunk.

And Ink Spot could be
As still as a fox,
But could jump up as fast
As a jack-in-the-box!

Slinking and clanking,

He would not stop to rest.

So Ink Spot the skunk

Got to be a big pest.

So on the skunk's neck

Bill hung a tin bell,

And if Ink Spot was bad,

Its ringing would tell.

Mrs. Kent's Trip

Mrs. Kent got up at sunup. She was going
to Miss West's and she had a lot to do.
She had to pack her trunk.

"Get going, get going, get going," she
said to herself. "Pack the trunk — pack
it fast!"

She began to pack the trunk. She put in:

a pink dress, a black dress, a tan dress,
six handbags, a sack of socks, ten hats,
a cap, a fan, a wig,
pins in a pinbox and pills in a pillbox,
a brass clock, a big map, a red cup,
a flag as a gift for Miss West,
a pink silk duck for luck,
a ham and a big pot to put it in,
and a glass jug of gumdrops.

Mrs. Kent had lots of stuff, and she put lots of stuff in the trunk. It was a big trunk.

At ten she sent for a cab. As she sat by the sink, drinking milk, the cabman rang the bell.

"O!" said Mrs. Kent. "It's YOU!"

"O!" said the cabman. "It's YOU!"

"Let's get going," said Mrs. Kent. "I want to go to Miss West's. You've got to put the trunk in your cab."

The cabman was blinking at the trunk. It was a big trunk.

"I'm not putting any clunking big trunk in my cab," he said.

"But what'll I do? I've got to have my trunk."

"Why not go to Miss West's on the bus? It'll fit in the bus."

"But will you get my trunk to the bus?" said Mrs. Kent.

"No, Mrs. Kent, I won't. You'll just have to get a van."

"A van! Just to get to the bus stop?" Mrs. Kent was yelling.

"Just to get to ANY stop! Why your trunk's as big as a tank. It'll fit in a van, but not in my cab."

"Couldn't you put a plank on top of the cab, Mr. Cabman? And put the trunk on the plank?"

"No," said the cabman.

"Well," said Mrs. Kent, "I've got to get going."

She sent for a van. The cabman sat by the sink, drinking milk.

The van man rang the bell.

"O!" said Mrs. Kent and the cabman. "It's YOU."

"O!" said the van man. "It's YOU. And YOU."

"Well," said the cabman, "let's get going. Mrs. Kent has to get her trunk to the bus stop. She and her trunk are going to Miss West's."

The van man was blinking at the trunk.

"You want the trunk to go on the bus?" he said.

"Yes, I do."

The van man began tugging and yanking at the trunk.

"What've you got in here, Mrs. Kent?" he said. "Rocks?"

"No," said Mrs. Kent. "Not rocks. Socks."

"It'll be a big job, getting it on the van," he said. "I'll have to get help."

"I'll help," said the cabman.

They began yanking and tugging. They put a plank up to the van. Huffing and puffing, tugging and yanking, banging and clanking, they got the trunk in the van.

"It CAN'T be socks," said the van man.

At the bus stop, huffing and puffing, tugging and yanking, they got the trunk off.

The bus man ran up. He was yelling, "No you don't, no you don't! You don't put a trunk on MY bus!"

"Yes, we do," said the cabman. "Mrs. Kent and her trunk are going to Miss West's. She's going on your bus."

"Well, her trunk isn't going on my bus," said the bus man. "Mrs. Kent, yes. The trunk, no."

Mrs. Kent began to yell. "What'll I do? What'll I do? I've got to get to Miss West's!"

"Well, don't yell at ME," said the bus man. "I can't help it if they don't let trunks on the bus. Who got the trunk here?"

"They did," said Mrs. Kent. "Mr. Cabman and Mr. Van Man."

"Well, they can get it to Miss West's," said the bus man.

"Why, so they can!" said Mrs. Kent. "Let's put it back on the van!"

"O, are you going to help, Mrs. Kent?" said the cabman, winking.

"No," said Mrs. Kent.

Well, they put it back. They put the plank up to the van, and huffing and puffing, tugging and yanking, banging and clanking, they got the trunk on the van.

The cabman and the van man and Mrs. Kent
herself began to sing:

"We're going, we're going, we're going!
We're off on a trip to Miss West's!
　We've got a big trunk,
　We put up a plank,
　We tug and we yank . . .
We did it, we did it, we did it!
We're off on a trip to Miss West's!"

But the bus man didn't sing.

"I just want to ask," he said, "why you didn't go to Miss West's from Mrs. Kent's? Why did you come here and yank the trunk off and have to put it back on? Why didn't you just go in the van and the cab?"

But they couldn't tell him.

They didn't know!

sh __

shall ▪ shack	shed ▪ shell ▪ shelf	shin ▪ ship ▪ shift	shop ▪ shot ▪ shock	shut

__ sh

cash	flesh	dish	slosh	gush
dash	fresh	fish		hush
rash		wish		mush
sash				rush
flash				blush
slash				flush
smash				slush
crash				brush
trash				crush
ash				

64

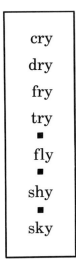

cry
dry
fry
try
■
fly
■
shy
■
sky

A cat was batting at a fly.

In a wink the fly was in the sky.

A pup ran by.

"Why try to hit the fly?" said
the pup.

"I can't hit it," said the cat.
"I'm shy. And I'm going to cry."

"Don't cry," said the pup, "or
you'll get wet. You want to be
dry. I know what: I'll bring you
an egg. You can fry it."

A Snack for a Cat

Bess the hen and Hank the duck were
the best of pals. They were going to
the hen's shed on the hilltop.

Step-step-step! In back of Hank
and Bess, a cat was slinking in the
brush.

"Wack, wack," said Hank. "A cat
is in back of us. She'll get us.
She must want us for a snack.
Come on! We've got to get to the shed!"

"Sh-sh-sh," said Bess.
"Let's not rush. She must be
going to the pond to get some fish.
She wouldn't want us."

"But she's a cat," said Hank. "And
cats don't fish. She MUST want US.
Cats are fast. She'll be here in
a flash and grab us. And what will be
left of us? We'll be two cat snacks!
What shall we do? What SHALL we do?"

And Hank began to cry.

"Hush, Hank, hush! Try not to cry,"
said Bess.

"We've got to rush, Bess!" said Hank.
"She's going to get us, I just know it.
I don't want to be a snack for any cat."

So Bess ran as fast as she could.
Would the cat want to snack on a duck
or a hen? She didn't know the cat, so
she couldn't tell.

"Stop, Bess, I have a plan," said
Hank. Hank was not crying. He
was trying to help.

"Here's my plan. We can go swimming in the pond in back of the shed," he said. "What cat wants to get wet? The cat won't come into the pond to get us."

"But I can't swim!" said Bess. "Your plan won't help me. Here is my plan. Grab some catnip from the bank. Bring it back and put it in the shed. The cat will smell the catnip and will go in to get it. If she gets the catnip, shut her in the shed."

Hank got some catnip and ran back to the shed. But in his rush he forgot the cat.

The cat was not slinking in the brush or rushing to the shed. She was just sitting still. Crash! Hank ran smack into her.

As Hank hid the catnip, the cat said, "I'm Flash. I'm glad I met you here. You and the hen ran so fast I couldn't stop you.

"I was trying to ask you to be my pals. I don't have many pals here. I wish I could have some cat pals. But I don't know any."

"I'm glad you don't want us as snacks," said Hank. "I'll be your pal."

Just as Hank said "pal," Bess was
dashing up to the shed to help him.
Swish! She was going so fast she couldn't
stop. And she went crash — into
the cat and Hank.

"Why, Hank," she said, "what are you
doing sitting next to the cat?"

"Hush!" said Hank. "We don't have to
trick the cat. Flash isn't going to snack
on us. She just wants us to be her pals."

"Well, Flash," said Bess, "I'm glad to
be your pal."

"Do you want some catnip?" said
Hank. Lifting it up on his wing, he
put it on the rock next to Flash.

Flash held up the catnip. "No, no,"
she said. "I couldn't have it just for
myself. You and Hank and I will have
the catnip."

"I'm not fond of catnip," said Bess.

"Catnip is not my dish," said Hank.
"But Bess and I can have a snack
if we go to the shed."

So off they went to have a snack.
Flash had pals at last.

Said a Duck . . .

Said a duck, just cracking her shell,

"I wish I could fly for a spell!"

She went FLAP! She went DASH!

She DID try, but went crash.

"What a shock!" said the duck as she fell.

Said the duck, rushing off to the pond,

"Of swimming I'll try to be fond.

If I'm wet, I shan't cry,

For I know I'm drip-dry,

So I'll slosh and I'll swish in the pond."

The Gruff King

King Gruff was the king of
a land in the West.

"I can do what I want. I can
have what I want. What I wish
will be so. I am the king,"
said King Gruff.

And so it was.

King Gruff kept a bell on
his desk. If he rang it, a man
would dash in to ask, "What
is your wish? Can I help you,
my king?"

The man would kiss the king's
ring, as the king had said he must
do. The king would clap his hands
and men would come rushing in to do
what he said.

Yet King Gruff was a sad man.
As fast as his men were, the king
would get mad and yell at them.
He would smash his fist on his desk.
And he would bang on his bell. The
king's men would do as the king said—
but they were not fond of him. They
left the king to himself.

As the gruff king sat by himself,
he said, "Men will jump if I yell.
They will rush in to me if I ring my
bell. They do what I wish, but still
I don't get what I want. My men have
left me. Not a man is a pal to me.
I don't know what to do." The king didn't
know he was so gruff.

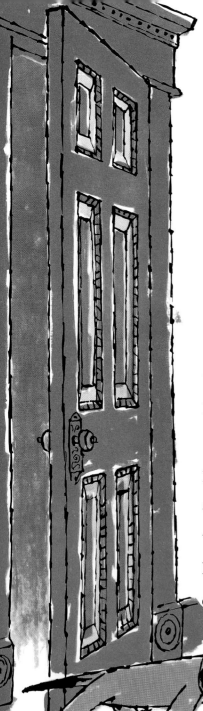

The sky was black and wet, and the king was sad. He didn't know what to do. So he went to his den to rest. As he was resting, a pup ran into the den. It was wet and had come in to get dry. It sat on the king's rug to rest.

"Who let that pup in?" the king said. "Get rid of it! Shut it up in the shed! Don't let it in here!"

But not a man was left to get the pup. And the pup didn't run off at the king's gruff yelling. It was trying to lick the king's hand. And the king could not bring himself to get rid of the wet pup.

"Isn't it odd?" said the king. "I didn't
tell the pup to kiss my ring. The pup
just did it — the pup WANTS to kiss my
ring. And it isn't running from me.
Why, it must be fond of me! I have a pal
at last and I didn't have to wish for it."

King Gruff was so glad he
began to grin.

"Why, I'm grinning," he said
to himself. "So I'm not sad.
You will be my pet."

King Gruff was still king,
but he was NOT still gruff.
He didn't bang on the desk
or yell. At last he didn't
have to sit by himself.

The pup sat on a mat
next to him. King Gruff
would sit and grin and pet
the pup.

And King Gruff's men began
to come back to him.

"He isn't King Gruff," they
said. "He's King Glad.
A pup did the trick."

A Fresh Fish for Two

If we had a fish from the fish shop,

As fresh as we could get,

We'd dry the fish and fry the fish,

Fresh from the shell or net.

O, we wish for some fish—a fish dish—

A dish of fresh fish for two!

And if we had cash, we would get some.

But I have no cash—have you?

Mrs. Bly Helps an Elf

At sunset Mrs. Bly shut up her shop.

"My, it's hot," she said to herself.

"I wish I didn't have to go back by bus.
I wish I could fly."

FLASH! SWISH!

"What was that flash?" Mrs. Bly began
to yell. "What was that swish? What's
going on here?"

"It's me!"

It was an elf! He was sitting on a
trash can, grinning at Mrs. Bly.

"I got here in a flash," he said.
"You said you had a wish, so here I am.
So! You wish you were a fly, do you?"

"No, no! I wasn't wishing to BE a fly.

I was wishing I COULD fly."

"Well," said the elf, "I could fix it.

I could fix it up in a flash, but . . ."

"But what? Won't you try?"

The sly elf said, "If I help you, you

must help me!"

"O, I will! I will!" said Mrs. Bly.

"What shall I do? What's your wish?"

"Um, gosh," said the elf. "You've got me. It's odd, but I just don't have any wish."

"But if you have no wish, I can't help you," said Mrs. Bly.

"And I can't help YOU," said the elf. "I'll just have to fly back to Elfland."

"No, no!" Mrs. Bly was yelling. "Don't rush off. We'll get you a wish. We must try. Come and let Mr. Bly fix us a snack. And we'll try to get you a wish."

"I don't know," said the elf. "I should be getting back."

"O, come on! Don't be shy. Mr. Bly will be so glad to know you."

"Well, O.K.," said the elf. "You can go by bus. I'm going to fly. I can do it in a flash."

FLASH! SWISH! And he was off.

On the bus, Mrs. Bly kept wishing she could fly. "The elf could help," she kept telling herself. "I wish HE had a wish! If I could just help him, he'd help me."

The elf was at the Blys' when she got off the bus. Mrs. Bly and the elf went in.

Mr. Bly was in back, fixing hash. He began yelling, "Is it you, Bess?"

"Yes," said Bess Bly. "And I'm bringing an elf. Can you let us have a snack?"

Mr. Bly got mad. "An elk!" he began to yell. "I don't want any elk in here. Elks are big. Elks bash and crash! Elks are a mess! I didn't fix my best hash for any elk! Get rid of the elk. Tell the elk to . . ."

"Not an elk, Bill. An ELF!" said Mrs. Bly. "Here he is. Can't we have a snack?"

Mr. Bly began blushing. "O," he said. "An elf! What fun! We're so glad to have you, Elf. Come in and sit!"

The elf did. He sat on a pot of shamrocks that Mr. Bly kept on a shelf.

"Can we have a snack, Bill?" said Mrs. Bly.

"O, my!" said Mr. Bly. "I was just frying some hash. But hash won't do for an elf. I'll fix him some . . ."

But the elf began sniffing. "What do
I smell?" he said. "It smells swell,
Mr. Bly."

"It's the hash," Mr. Bly said.

"It IS swell," said Mrs. Bly. "Bill's
hash is the best."

"What's hash?" said the elf.

"What's hash?" said Mrs. Bly. "Haven't
you had hash? Why, hash is a tidbit fit
for a king!"

The elf was sniffing and sniffing.

"We don't have hash in Elfland," he
said. "Let me try it, Mr. Bly."

Mr. Bly set a dish of hot hash on the
shelf by the elf.

The elf went hopping off the
shamrock. He went dashing to the dish.
He had a bit of hash.

"Yum!" he said. "O, yum, yum, YUM!
O, hash, hash, HASH! Hash is swell!
I wish we had hash in Elfland!"

"You WISH it?" said Mrs. Bly. "So
you DO have a wish! And I can fix it up
for you. If Mr. Bly helps you to mix
up a pan of hot hash, will you help me
to fly?"

"YES!" said the elf.

So, if you smell a yum-yum smell in
Elfland, it's the elf frying hash for
his pals.

And if you spot Mrs. Bly in the sky—

well, you know why. She's going to the

shop, and not by bus.

FLASH! SWISH!

It's Mrs. Bly flying by!

th__					
thank		thin ∎ think ∎ thing ∎ thick		thump

__th					
bath path	Beth tenth	with Smith ∎ fifth ∎ sixth		

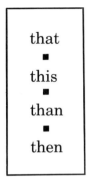

that
■
this
■
than
■
then

"What's <u>this</u>, Beth?" said Mr. Smith.

"<u>That</u> is a big red box, Dad," said Beth.

<u>Then</u> Mr. Smith held up a pink box.

"Do you think <u>that</u> <u>this</u> box has less

in it <u>than</u> the red box?"

"I can't tell," said Beth. "The pink

box is not as big as the red box. But

a big box could still have less in it."

"<u>That</u> is so," said her dad. "The red box

could have less in it <u>than</u> the pink box."

The Fish and the Bat

Swish was a fish who could swim
as fish do. She swam in a pond.
Swish would think as she swam, and
she was sad. For she would think of
the sky. She would think to herself,
"I wish, I wish I could fly!"

Thump was a black bat. And,
as you know, bats can fly.

Well, at sunset, Thump would
fly in the sky by Swish's pond.

Thump was as sad as Swish.
He was thinking, "I wish I
could swim! I wish I were
in the pond."

Flapping his wings, Thump
said, "This sky is so dry and
the pond is so wet! Why can't
I swim?"

Thump sat on a twig next to the pond to rest. As Thump sat, Swish swam past him.

Thump was getting to know Swish. On Swish's fifth trip by, Thump said, "Fish! Fish! Do you think I could try to swim?"

"What's that? You're a bat," said Swish. "You can fly in the sky! Why should you want to swim?"

"The sky is so dry and your
pond is so wet," said Thump.
"That is why I want to swim
in your pond."

"No!" said Swish. "A pond isn't
as big as the sky. Why should
you want to swim in this pond?
A pond is just a big bathtub. I
wish I could fly with the wind
as you do."

Swish kept swimming past, and
the two kept thinking. On Swish's
tenth swim past Thump, Swish said,
"I'd be glad to help you swim, if
you'd help me fly."

"Yes. Yes. I'll help you fly,"
said Thump.

"Come on into my pond then,"
said Swish.

Plop! Thump was in the pond,
and he began to flap his wings.

"No, no!" said Swish. "Don't flap your wings." So Thump didn't.

But Thump began to sink. His wings didn't help him, and he sank fast. He couldn't swim. He felt sick. Swish had to help him get back up to the top.

"I can't swim as you do," said Thump. Swish felt sad for Thump, but she couldn't help him swim. Was swimming something that just fish could do?

Thump was on the bank, flapping
his wet wings to get them dry.
"It's fun to fly in the sky," he
said. "I think I should help you
fly, Swish. Come with me, and
I'll help you get up to the sky.
The sky is dry. It isn't a bathtub."

"Let's go," said Swish. "I'll try my
best to fly." And up they went.

The sky was big and black to Swish,
and the wind stung her. The sky was
dry, not wet as her pond was. Swish
felt ill.

"I wish I could be back in my pond
so I could go swimming," said Swish.
"I can't swim up here in the sky."

"Then let go, Swish. Let go!" said
the bat.

Swish let go and fell back into the
pond.

"Thank you! Thank you!" said
Swish. "I'm so glad to be wet. I'm
so glad that I can swim!"

"And I'm so glad to be dry," said
Thump. "I'm so glad I can fly."

Do you know what? They were
glad they had met at the pond.

I Think I'll Be

I think I'll be a fish

    That can swim in a dish.

Or should I be a bug,

    With a nest in a rug?

I think I'll be an elf,

    Not as big as myself.

Or I could be a king,

    Who can do just anything!

I think I'll be a frog,

    And thump on a log.

And the sixth thing I'll be?

    Why—I think I'll be ME!

Dad's Rest

Dad had a bath and then he had
a glass of milk.

"I think I'll rest till Mom gets
back," he said. "Trish and Beth,
will you do the things Mom said you
should do? I want to have a nap."

"O.K., Dad," said Trish and Beth.
"And we'll be still so you can rest."

"Thanks," said Dad. Then off he went
for a nap.

Beth got her dress and began to fix
the hem on it.

"I think I'll get Smith some milk,"
said Trish. Smith was Trish's cat.

But just as she was getting the milk,
the bell rang. It was Cliff, a pal.

"Come in, Cliff," said Beth. "What
can we do for you?"

"I've come to ask you for something,"
said Cliff. "Do you have any junk that
you want to get rid of?"

"We have lots of junk that you can have," said Trish. "But hush! Dad's resting."

As Trish said that, Beth was getting a box of junk off a shelf. She had to get up on a cot to lift it. CRASH! SMASH! THUMP! The box fell.

"Beth, be still! You know Dad is resting," said Trish. "I'll help you pick up this junk and put it back in the box."

She did. Then she said, "Cliff, here it is."

"Thanks a lot," said Cliff as he left.

"That's O.K.," said Trish.

Beth went back to fixing the hem of her dress.

"No singing! No jumping! No thumping! We'll be still as rocks so Dad can rest," she said.

Beth and Trish WERE still, but not the cat. It began to yelp.

"What's that?" said Beth at the top of her lungs. "Smith is yelling for help."

Just then Smith ran by as fast
as he could go. In back of the cat
ran a big dog, yelping as it went.
Trish held on to the lamp as the cat
and dog went dashing by. The cat slid
into a clock, and the dog hit a
stack of blocks.

CRASH! BANG! THUMP!

"What a mess!" said Beth.

"I'll bet Dad is upset," said Trish.

"Hush!" said Beth. "I'll fix the
clock, and you pick up the blocks."

Just as Beth put the dog in the shed,
two of Beth's pals began to yell for
her. Shel and Bess were on the path
yelling for Beth to help ring some
bells that they had.

CLING-CLANG! CLANG-CLANG!
The bells were ringing.

"Hush!" said Trish and Beth, but
they did not know what to do. They
ran to Dad. They felt that he would
be up, and he was. They were going
to tell him that they just couldn't help it.

"Dad! You're . . . you're . . . up!"
Trish began.

"Dad! We're so . . ." Beth began.

Dad had a hug and a grin for
Trish and Beth.

"No, I couldn't rest," he said.
"What a lot of fussing!"

"You must be mad at us,"
said Trish and Beth.

"No," said Dad, "I'm not. I forgot
that I had to go to the bus stop to
get Mom. So I'm thanking you. But
come on! You can come."

And they went off to pick up Mom.

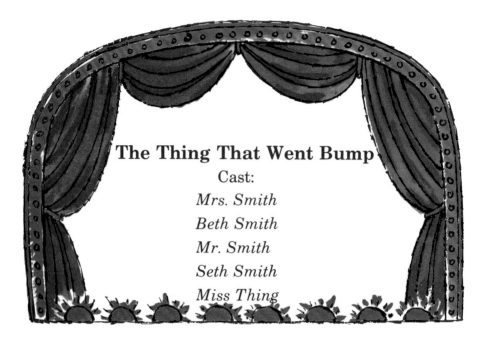

The Thing That Went Bump

Cast:

Mrs. Smith

Beth Smith

Mr. Smith

Seth Smith

Miss Thing

Mrs. Smith: It's ten to six, Beth. I think
you should go and have your bath. And
then you must do your math.

Beth: O, Mom! Do I have to?

Mrs. Smith: Yes, you have to. Let's not
have any fussing.

Beth: Well, O.K. If I must . . .

Mr. Smith: Hush! What was that thump?

Beth: What thump?

Mr. Smith: That thump in back, just then,

as your mom was telling you

to have your bath. Didn't you . . .

Seth: Hush, Dad! It's still doing it!

Mrs. Smith: Yes! Something in back is

bumping and crashing.

(Mr. Smith runs off.)

Beth: I didn't get a hint of a bump

or crash or anything.

Seth: Gosh, Beth! You would if you'd try!

That was the fifth crash! I think it

was on the path in back. O! You couldn't

miss THAT!

That was the sixth!

Beth: No, I didn't miss that! That was a

big crash! What's going on?

Mrs. Smith: I don't know. But it's got me

upset. I can't help thinking of . . .

well, you know . . . theft and so on.

Beth: I don't think it could be that, Mom.

If some man were trying to rob us, he

wouldn't go banging and thumping. He'd

be as still as he could.

Seth: Here comes Dad. He's back.

Beth: And he's not by himself.

(Mr. Smith and Miss Thing come in.)

Mrs. Smith: What was it? Was it something

on the path? And who's that with you?

Mr. Smith: This is Miss Thing — Miss Meg Thing.

She was on the path.

Mrs. Smith: Glad to know you, Miss Thing.

Was that you, bumping and thumping?

(Miss Thing nods.)

What were you doing?

Seth: Yes, tell us.

Miss Thing: I was jumping. I do a lot
of jumping.

Mr. Smith: Why do you do that?

Miss Thing: Jumping keeps me fit, as you
can see. I began jumping to keep
fit. I got fit jumping. So then I
kept on jumping, just for the fun
of it. I'm glad I got fit, but I will
not stop jumping. If I did, then I
wouldn't have a tenth of the fun that I do.

Mrs. Smith: What an odd thing to do to have
fun. IS jumping fun?

Miss Thing: Fun? Is jumping FUN? Let me

tell you! You should just try jumping

the width of your back path. That's

what I was doing. If you'd try it,

you'd know what fun it is! That path

has a lot of width to it, so you get a

smashing big thump at the end. Why not

try it, Mrs. Smith? It IS fun.

Mrs. Smith: O, I couldn't do that!

Miss Thing: Why not?

Mrs. Smith: Well, it just isn't the thing

to do! It's odd! Don't get mad, but I

think it's just nuts!

Beth: O, come on, Mom. It COULD be fun.

So what if it's odd?

Seth: Yes, Mom. Let's try. So what if it's

nuts? Who will know?

Mrs. Smith: Well, O.K. then. Let's try.

Mr. Smith (grinning): You run and jump, and

then you thump. Is that it, Miss Thing?

Miss Thing: That's it, Mr. Smith.

Seth: Let's go, Beth. Let's do it.

Beth: O.K.! Let's jump and bump and thump.

It can't be bad if it lets me put off

my bath and my math!

The Smiths and Miss Thing (jumping, jumping,

jumping):

We'll run! We'll jump!
We'll end with a thump!
   For jumping and bumping are fun!
If you think that it's mad,
Well, just try — it's not bad,
In the fog or in the sun.

We'll dash! We'll crash!
We'll end with a smash!
   And we know it's odd to you.
But if dashing and crashing
And bashing are fun,
   They COULD be the things to do, to do,
      They could be the things to do.

(The Smiths and Miss Thing go jumping off. The rest is just a lot of thumps and bumps.)

This and That

Do that, do this,

Do this, do that.

 Thank your Dad.

 Pick up your hat.

 Go to bed.

 Have your bath.

 Kiss your Mom.

 Do your math.

 Drink your milk.

 Skip on the path.

Do that, do this,

Do this, do that.

I think that I'll get big, and then

I can tell this and that to them.

     And I WILL!

Who's Who?

Thick was the twin of her twin, who was Thin.

And Thin was the twin of Thick.

Twin Thick was as thick as a thumping fat stick,

And Thin was as thin as a pin.

Then Thick got sick – but not her twin.

Twin Thin was well, not sick.

So Thick began thinning, till she was as thin

As Thin was. But Thin got thick!

Well, Thin is still the twin of Thick,

But Thin is thick, not thin.

And Thick is not thick, for she was so sick.

What a trick! Is Thin Thick and Thick Thin?

ch___

chap ■ chat	check ■ chest	chin ■ chip ■ chick ■ chill	chop	chug ■ chum ■ Chuck

___ch

ranch	bench	rich ■ pinch inch		much such ■ bunch lunch punch

mother
brother
other
another
■
father
■
done
one

Miss King said to Chuck, "Do you have a brother?"

"My twin is my brother," said Chuck.

"Do you have another brother?" said Miss King.

"Yes," said Chuck. "I have one other, my big brother, Chet."

"Any other?" said Miss King.

"No, just the two of them. And I have my mother and my father," said Chuck.

"Well done!" said Miss King.

Cat in the Jam Pot

We said to one another,
"Did anyone tell Mother?
Did anyone tell Mother
 that the cat is in the jam?"

"Not me," said Sam, my brother.
"Well, you should have run to Mother."
I said, "You could STILL tell Mother."
 (That is what I said to Sam.)

And I said to Sam, my brother,
"Did anyone tell Father?
Did anyone tell Father
 that the cat is in it, Sam?"

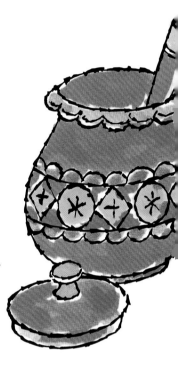

Sam said, "YOU should go tell Father.

Someone HAS to go tell Father.

Cats should not get into jam pots

and go munching on the jam."

We went and got the others —

Chuck and Rich (two other brothers) —

And we said, "Will one of you two

tell them she is in the pot?"

Chuck said, "Rich should go tell Father."

Rich said, "Chuck could go tell Mother."

I said, "Have we got another brother?"

Sam said, "I think not."

"But what's that?" said Rich, my brother.

And with grins at one another,

We said, "It's the cat herself, and

    she is licking off. She's done!

"No one here, not any brother,

Has to dash and yell to Mother!

No one has to go tell Father!

    No, not us, not anyone!

    She is DONE!"

What's for Lunch?

Beth and Chuck were digging in the sandbox, and they weren't thinking of lunch. But Father had come to get them.

"Chuck! Beth!" said Father. "We are going to have lunch. Stop digging and come in."

So Chuck and Beth left the sandbox and went in. They could smell fish frying in a pan.

"What do you think we'll have
for lunch?" Chuck said to Beth.

"I want ham and eggs," said Beth,
with her chin in her hands.

"What do you want for lunch, Chuck?"

Chuck said, "I want this and that."

Beth said, "What's this and that?"

"Well," Chuck said, grinning, "do you
think Father is frying frogs' wings
for us?"

"Frogs don't have wings," Beth said.

"Is he chopping up a cobweb?"
Chuck said.

"Can you chop up a cobweb?"
said Beth.

"Well," Chuck said, "I want Father
to fix me a cobweb sandwich
and one bunch of frogs' wings."

Beth began to grin. "Would you
want to add a bunch of tin figs
to that lunch?" she said.

"That would be swell," Chuck said.
"Can you think of any other things?"

Beth began to think, and at
last she said, "Yes, I think I'd
add a pinch of fresh mist. You're
next, Chuck."

"I'd wish for a box of huffs
and puffs," Chuck said. "And an
inch of hot red and black dots."

Beth said, "I have another! I want pink
ranch punch and a chest of sunset chips!"

But Father had come in.

"I think you two have a lot of pep,"
he said. "Come and have your lunch."

"What will we have?" Beth said.

"Well," said Father, "what do
you want? Do you want a lunch box of
tick-tock buns or a yum-yum sandwich
with a pinch of buzz-fuzz?"

Beth and Chuck began to grin.

Beth said, "It's fun, isn't it?"

"Yes, it's fun," Father said. "But you won't get much of a lunch if you get what you're wishing for. Your lunch will just have to be a dish of fresh fish, a drink of milk, and a bunch of figs."

"I smell it," Beth said.

"And I smell it," Chuck said.

And Beth said to Father, "That's just the lunch we want."

"Yes," Chuck said. "That's what we want."

Chip Is My Chum

Chip is my chum. He asks me why
    A fish can swim but cannot fly.
And why a bug that has two wings
    Can fly but can't do other things.

He asks so much, I want to cry,
    "Why must you ask me, WHY, WHY, WHY?"
Chip's my chum, yes he's my brother.
    Another "Why?" and I'll ask Mother.

Jet and His Pal

Jet was a pup, and Scat was a fat cat.
They were chums. They did things that
chums do with one another. If Jet
had his lunch, the fat cat had
her lunch. If Scat had milk, Jet
had milk. If Jet sat on a bench,
Scat sat on the bench with him.
They were chums and that was that!

But the best of chums have
to have something to do.

"What SHALL we do?" Scat
was asking.

"Come on," said Jet. "Let's go
sit on the grass by the pond."

"Swell!" said the fat cat. And off
they went, up the path to the pond.

A duck was swimming on the pond.
She swam up and back on the pond.
She swam past Jet the pup and Scat
the fat cat.

As she was swimming past,

the duck sang:

"Dogs and cats have lots of spats,

But Scat is fond of Jet.

Why this is so

I do not know.

For he will nip her yet."

The fat cat said, "What's the

duck singing?"

But Jet the pup didn't think the
fat cat should know what the duck
was singing. So he said, "She's just
singing to the sun. Come on, Scat. Let's
run on the grass!"

So the fat cat and Jet had
fun running on the grass. But
the duck was still swimming
in the pond, up and back, past
the bank. And as she swam
she sang:

"Dogs and cats have lots of spats,

But Scat is fond of Jet.

Why this is so

I do not know.

For he will nip her yet."

"That duck is still singing," said
the fat cat. "What is she singing?"

"She's singing for her mother and
father," said the pup. "Come on, Scat.
Let's jump on the grass and then we
can go back."

But the fat cat ran to the pond. "Come here, duck," she said. "What are you singing?"

Sang the duck:

"Dogs and cats have lots of spats,

But Scat is fond of Jet.

Why this is so

I do not know.

For he will nip her yet."

Scat ran back to Jet. She
was in a huff. Jet began to run,
for he didn't know what Scat would
do. Would the fat cat still be his chum?
Scat ran to the pond. But she was
running so fast she couldn't stop.
And plop! In she went!

"Help!" she was yelling, for she could
not swim. But Jet could swim. In two
jumps he was in the pond and he swam to
help his chum. He got Scat by the back
of the neck and swam back to land.
At last Scat was back on the grass.

"Thank you, Jet," she said.

"Any pup that would do what
you did must be my chum."

And the duck sang:

"Jet's a chum of Scat the cat,

But he is not her brother.

If one of them

Should want some help,

He just yells for the other."

Shopping for Fun

Ann and her brother Chip had
had lunch.

"That was such a big lunch, I think
we should just sit and rest," said Ann.

"It isn't fun just to sit," said Chip.

"What do you want to do, Ann? Sit
and rest or have some fun?"

"Well, I want to have fun," said Ann.
"What do you think we should do?
Do you have any plans?"

"No," said Chip. "But I'll think of
something. You must sit and think
with me. Let's try to think of
something we haven't done yet."

As Chip and Ann were thinking,

Mother was fixing some punch. Ann and Chip didn't know that Mother was thinking of them.

At last Ann said to Chip, "I can't think of one thing to do."

Then Chip said to Ann, "I can't think of anything that's fun."

"Well, I can!" said Mother with a grin. "You can help me by going shopping for me."

"But MOTHER!" said Chip with
a gasp. "Ann and I were trying to think
of something that would be FUN!"

"This will be fun," said his mother.

"Shopping isn't fun," said Chip as
he drank a glass of punch.

"Come on," said Ann. "Let's do it.
We can't think of anything that's fun.
So let's help Mom."

"Here's a list of things for you to
get," said Mother. "I must go." And
she left.

"I wish we didn't have to shop," said Chip. "And how CAN we shop? WE don't have any cash."

"Well, we said we would, so we MUST," said Ann. "Here's the list."

Chip held the list. Here's what it said:

1. Get something that rings.

2. Get something to drink.

3. Get something to munch on.

4. Get something to sit on.

5. Get something for lunch.

6. Get something that swims.

"But that isn't telling us what she wants," said Ann. "Mother said she'd tell us what to get and we still don't know."

"Yes we do," said Chip. "Mother wants us to think. And we don't have to have cash. We'll go shopping, but not in a shop. Let's try, Ann. We'll have fun."

"O.K.!" said Ann. "I'll do 1, 2, and 3, and you do 4, 5, and 6. And then we'll come back and put the things on the bench." And off they went.

Ann and Chip had to go to many odd spots. They went as fast as they could.

At last they got back. They were
huffing and puffing so much, they
had to sit and rest.

"I got just what Mom put on the
list!" said Chip with a grin.

"And so did I!" said Ann.

Just as they put the things on
the bench, the bell rang. It was
Mother.

"Mother! Mother!" they began to yell.
"We have the six things on the list!
They are here on this bench!"

"You DO!" she said with a grin.

"I didn't think you could do it.

WHAT things did you get?"

"Here is the list, Mom," said Ann.

"You can check it off as we go."

Mom held the list in one hand and a

pen in the other hand.

She said, "What did you get that
rings?"

"My clock!" said Ann. "It rings to
get me up!"

Mom put a check next to the 1.

"What did you get that you can
drink?" said Mom.

"Punch," said Ann. "Some was
left in Chip's glass."

Mom put a check next to the 2.

"What did you get to munch on?" said Mom.

"Some nuts in a dish," said Ann. "You had left some on the top shelf."

Mom put a check next to the 3.

"Well, what did you get to sit on?" said Mom.

"I got a bench, Mom," said Chip.
"I got the one Ann's doll sits on!"

Mom put a check next to the 4.

"What did you get that we could have for lunch?" said Mom.

"I got a bunch of plums," said Chip.

"I did a job for Mr. Smith in his shop. I got the plums for doing the job!"

Mom put a check next to the 5.
Then she began to grin.

"I didn't think you could get
this last one," she said. "What
could you get that swims? And the bench
hasn't got six things on it."

Chip was grinning so much he
couldn't tell Mom. But—HE sat on
the bench.

"I can swim, Mom," said Chip.
"And I am the sixth thing on the
bench!"

"Did you have fun?" said Mom.

"Did you?" said Ann and Chip.
Well, did they?

155

What Is an Inch?

Can you tell me what an inch is?

Is it thin or is it thick?

Is it something I can munch on?

Can it fly or can it kick?

I cannot think what it can be.

    Is it something you can pinch?

I think that I'll ask my father

    If he'll let me have an inch.

__tch					
catch	fetch	ditch		Dutch
hatch	sketch	pitch		clutch
latch	stretch	witch		crutch
match		stitch		
patch		switch		
snatch		itch		

158

wh__					
	wham ■ whack	when	whip ■ which ■ whiff ■ whisk		

qu__					
	quack		quit ■ quiz ■ quilt ■ quick		

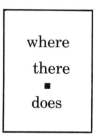

where

there

■

does

"Where are you going?" said

Bill to Ann.

"I'm going to shop," said Ann.

"Does Mom know that you're

going to shop?" said Bill.

"Yes," said Ann. "She sent me

to get some fish."

"I'll go with you," said Bill.

"I'll help you bring the fish back.

Will there be fish for lunch?"

"No, it isn't for us. But Mom

does want a fish for the cat."

"Where will you get it?" said Bill.

"At the fish shop," said Ann.

Ann Gets the Milk

"I don't have any milk for lunch, Ann," said Mrs. Chen. "The milk truck hasn't come yet. I think it's in the next block. Will you run to the truck and get us some milk? If you're quick, I think you'll catch the truck."

Ann got off the bench where she was sitting, and put on her cap. "I'll try my best, Mother," she said as she ran off.

She ran as fast as she could.
When she got to the next block,
there was the milk truck, stuck
in a ditch. Mr. Smith was in
the truck trying to get it to go.

"My truck hit a rock,"
said Mr. Smith. "It's stuck in
the mud. Will you help me, Ann?"

Ann said she'd be glad to help.

"What shall we do, Mr. Smith?"
said Ann.

"I think we'll have to try some
sticks and twigs," he said.

"We can put them in the ditch. When
I run the truck on the sticks and twigs,
the truck won't sink into the mud."

Mr. Smith and Ann went up
a hill to get some sticks and twigs.
They began to huff and puff as
they were lugging them to the ditch.
But they got them there. Then Mr.
Smith got back into his truck
to try to get it going.

Thump! Thump! Slish! Slosh!

The truck ran onto the sticks.
The truck went up and back,
up and back. At last it left the ditch.

"The truck is going! The truck is
going! We did the trick!" Ann was
yelling.

"Thank you for your help, Ann,"
said Mr. Smith. "I don't know what
I would've done if you hadn't come to
help."

"I was glad to help," said Ann.

Mr. Smith went off in the truck,

and Ann ran back to her mother.

When she got back she had to tell

Mrs. Chen what she had done.

"The truck was stuck. . . . I had
to get sticks. . . . And the truck slid
on the twigs and sticks. . . ."

Ann was rushing on so she wouldn't
forget anything.

"And Mr. Smith said 'Thank you'
to me, Mom. He said I was a big help
to him," Ann said.

"I am glad you were such a help

to Mr. Smith," said Mrs. Chen.

"But you forgot to help ME."

"What did I forget, Mother?" said Ann.

Mrs. Chen was grinning. "You forgot to

bring me any MILK," she said.

The Clock

I have a big clock
  That sits on a shelf.
When I am not there,
  It just ticks to itself.

But what is it for?
  I don't have to ask.
The clock tells me when
  I should do my next task.

If I have stitching
  In my mending kit,
I know when to do it
  And when I must quit.

I have a big clock.
  YOU'D think it went "Tick,"
But to me, with my tasks,
  It's going "Quick! Quick!"

What Can You Do?

Can you catch a pitch?
Yes, I can catch a pitch.

Can you dig a ditch?
Yes, I can dig a ditch.

Can you stitch a patch?
Yes, I can stitch a patch.

Can you snatch a switch?
Yes, I can snatch a switch.

Can you mix some punch?
Yes, I can mix some punch.

Can you bend a brick?
No, that would be a trick.

169

Miss Quick-Quack

1

Miss Quick-Quack, the Witch of
Westland, was going to her hut on
the hilltop.

Her back was bent and she was
limping. She went up the path with
the help of a crutch. But Patch,
her big black cat, was not as quick
as Miss Quick-Quack. He was whacking
at something by the path.

As she went, Miss Quick-Quack was
thinking of her one BIG wish.

"I wish I didn't have to be
a witch. But I can't help myself, for,
as anyone knows, a witch must
have a ring to cast a spell. And I don't
have a ring."

The King of Westland did not want
any spells cast in his land. So he had
said that no witch could have a ring.

Miss Quick-Quack sat on a log
to rest and to let Patch catch
up with her.

"Come, Patch, we must go up to the
hut. The sun is setting," she said.

But still Patch didn't come.

He was still snatching at something
in the grass.

"What do you have?" said Miss
Quick-Quack as she got up. "What
are you clutching?"

Miss Quick-Quack went to the
ditch.

What Patch was clutching was
not a bug or a rock or a rat. It was
a ring!

Miss Quick-Quack bent to pick
up the ring. Then she held it up
in the sunset. It began to flash.

"I know what it is," she said.
"It's the king's ring! Come on, Patch!
We've got to get to the hut as quick
as a flash!"

Limping, Miss Quick-Quack
went up to the hut on the hilltop.
Thump, thump, thump went the
crutch on the path.

Slam! She shut herself and Patch in the hut. Click went the latch.

"At last I have a ring," she said. "And it's the king's ring! At last I can cast a spell!"

As fast as she could, she got a match and some logs. She put a big black pot on the logs.

"I have a plan, but I must act fast," she said. "What if the king should come and catch me with his ring?"

2

Humming and grinning, Miss
Quick-Quack began to fill the pot
with things she kept just for spells.

Here is what she put in the pot:

    the hop of a frog,

    the sting of a bug,

    the itch of a sting,

    the drip of a drop,

    the chill of a fog,

    the flick of a whip,

and last,

    the tick of a clock.

Grinning and singing, Miss
Quick-Quack sat by the pot. She
held the king's ring, and began
to cast her spell.

"Trick-Track," she said.

But what was that? Many
men were in the glen. The
king's men were hunting for the
missing ring. They were coming up
to her hut!

"Quick-Quack, be quick!" she
said to herself. "You must try
to cast your spell. Trick-Track,
Trick-Track . . ."

But the king's men were up
to the path that led to the hut!
She must cast her spell, or they
would get into the hut and stop
her.

Would she get to cast the spell? The
men were at the end of the path!

"Trick-Track, Trick-Track . . ."

Bang, bang! The men were at
the hut. They were trying to
get in. But the latch held. Miss
Quick-Quack could still try to
cast the spell.

She put the ring in her left

hand and sang:

"Pitch-Patch!

Smitch-Smatch!

Bring my wish,

And help me switch

To someone who

Is not a witch!"

CRASH! SMASH!

The king's men were mad. Just as

they were going to smash the latch,

there was a cry. There were gasps.

And puff! The latch was melting.

The men went in. But what was this! There was no bent witch in the drab hut. There was just a lass.

"Why, where is the witch?" said the men.

"I am the witch," said the lass, with a shy blush. "I am Quick-Quack of Westland."

"Well, Miss Quick-Quack, we are the king's men. You haven't met anyone with a ring that can flash in the sun, have you? The king's ring is missing. It fell from his hand when he was hunting."

"A ring such as this?" said Miss Quick-Quack, as she held up the king's ring.

"THERE it is," said the men. "But where was it? We were hunting for it from sunup to sunset, and the ring was nowhere."

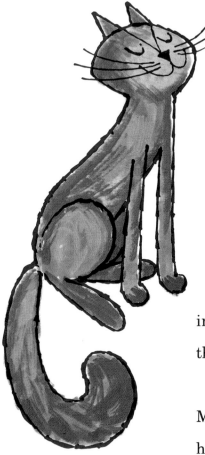

"My cat, Patch, was catching bugs in a ditch," she said. "The ring was there in the grass."

"The king will want to thank you, Miss," said the men. "He will let you have your wish. Think of what you want to wish for, so you can tell him."

"I don't have to think much," said Miss Quick-Quack. "I have had my wish. But let me go with you to the king. I must tell him that some spells are not bad."

3

So the men led Miss Quick-Quack to the king.

"Who are you bringing here?" said the king.

"It is Miss Quick-Quack, the witch," said one of the men. "She had your ring."

"No!" said the king. "That
lass can't be Miss Quick-Quack,
the witch!"

"Yes," she said. "I am Quick-Quack."

"The WITCH?" he said.

"I WAS the witch," said Miss
Quick-Quack.

"Then I thank you for my ring,
Miss Quick-Quack," said the king.
"You will get one wish. What
will it be?"

"King of Westland," said Miss Quick-Quack, "I have had my wish. It was my wish to stop being a witch and to be as others are."

She went on: "Thanks to you, I could not switch. You would not let any witch have a ring. Yet I had to have one to cast my last spell."

"Your last spell?" said the king.

"Yes," she said. "With your ring, I have cast it. And at last I have got my wish. I am NOT a witch. I am not Miss Quick-Quack. At last I am just Beth!"

"Well, Beth," said the king, "I am glad. Here is my ring. It is yours. And if you will wed me, you can have anything you want!"

Well! Beth had to think. She had her wish. She was glad just to be Beth. Should she wed the king as well?

"Let me think on it," she said.

"I will let you think on it," said the king. "But I won't stop asking. I'll ask you till you tell me yes."

Do you think Beth said yes? Would YOU have said yes?